KINGDOM BUILDERS IN BUSINESS

WRITTEN BY
JOAN T RANDALL
and ANGELA M HAIGLER

KINGDOM BUILDERS IN BUSINESS WORKBOOK

Published by Victorious You

Copyright @ 2020 Joan T Randall

All rights reserved

No part of this book may be reproduced, distributed, or transmitted in any form by any means, graphic, electronic, or mechanical, including photocopy, recording, taping, or by any information storage or retrieval system, without permission in writing from the publisher, except in the case of reprints in the context of reviews, quotes, or references.

Printed in the Unites States of America

Printed in the Unites States of America

First Printing, 2020

ISBN: 978-1-7340609-2-8

For details email Joan T Randall

joan@joantrandall.com or call 980-785-4959

www.joantrandall.com

HOW TO USE THIS WORKBOOK

The Kingdom Builders in Business Workbook is the companion guide to the Kingdom Builders in Business Anthology. It is geared towards study, taking action, and reflection - whether you choose to use it personally or as part of a book club or bible study group.

There are twelve stories in the Anthology and twelve study guide exercises in this workbook that correlate to each account. Read each story and then proceed to answer the questions for that story. For example, in Chapter 1, O is for Obedience; read Tami's story and then move to the workbook section for Chapter 1.

Find the similarities between you and each of the Authors and be as honest as possible in every response. Each chapter has biblical references that you can apply to your daily life.

There is plenty of space to write, and at the end of every chapter, there is an entire page for Personal Reflections. Use those spaces any way you want. You can write, draw, doodle images, or be as creative as you want to be.

FOR PERSONAL USE

Use the questions and prompts in each chapter to discover and rediscover, the one thing that will always be true to you and you alone – your story.

Have the intentional deep dive look at your life, love, finances, and spirituality. Acknowledge the experiences that brought you here and feel empowered to take those next steps to be the best of who you are.

Fill the blank spaces with your words, your thoughts, and your reflections. Personalize this book and make it about you and your innermost expressions.

FOR BOOK CLUBS OR STUDY GROUPS:

- Encourage everyone to answer at least one question rather than having a single individual monopolize the conversations.
- Allow for silence between questions to give time for participants to formulate their thoughts.
- If someone answers with a Yes or No, encourage real responses. Ask then to Explain.
- Be quick to listen and slow to give advice. Make sure the atmosphere is inclusive and non-judgmental.

Be Blessed.

CHAPTER 1
O IS FOR OBEDIENCE

Tami had been provided many messages from God. Not until she decided to obey those messages did her life begin to turn around. She gained strength and was able to connect to her true calling.

REVIEW

What did you connect with the most from Tami's story? Why did that section resonate with you? Share a moment when something similar happened to you.

TALK IT OUT

- Have there been times when you have heard something from God, but ignored it?

- Talk about a time when you felt left out and/or less than. What did you do about it?

PERSONALIZE IT

- **Read John 14:23 (NIV).** Obedience is being willing to let God set the direction when you don't know the details. What directions did God give you recently? What's the hardest part about obeying for you and why?

- **Proverbs 3: 5-6 (KJV).** In this passage, we are encouraged to trust God before ourselves. Compare and contrast times in your life when you took on a task, bypassing God to make something happen, only to become frustrated and stagnant. How did it feel when you allowed God to take the lead? What lessons did you learn?

TAKE ACTION

Where are you now in the process of being obedient? What do you need to release in order to trust and obey God?

Once I raised my hands in complete obedience, submitting my will and asking for the Lord's will to be done in my life, everything started to fall in place. I am grateful for the path the Lord has allowed me to follow and cross on this journey. If it were not for all of my experiences along the way, I would not be the strong woman I am today. –**Tami L Stewart**

PERSONAL REFLECTIONS

CHAPTER 2
REBORN

Throughout her life, Renée felt rejected and unloved by her mother. It took several "rebirths" before she realized God loved her, and her life was engraved on the palm of His hand. With that understanding, she pushed through her pain until she discovered her gifts from the Kingdom.

REVIEW

What did you connect with the most from Renée's story? Why did that section resonate with you? Share a moment when something similar happened to you.

TALK IT OUT

- In what ways have you ever felt unfulfilled, disappointed or emotionally absent from someone close to you?

- How has this impacted other relationships in your life?

PERSONALIZE IT

- **Read Isaiah 49:15-16 (NIV).** In these verses, Isaiah reminds us that God will never forsake us. What emotions does this passage evoke? How has God shown up in your life to prove that He is the ultimate comforter?

- **Psalm 118:22 (NIV).** Rejection can sometimes cause us pain and sorrow. These verses remind us that while man may forsake you, God never will. Create an affirmation that reflects God's love for you. Place it somewhere you can see it and recite it daily.

TAKE ACTION

Write a prayer to God about what you would like for him to do in your life this year regarding the relationship mentioned in the Talk it Out section.

As I lift my head in the stage of my life where wisdom has kicked in, I've learned that the Creator equips us with gifts wrapped in purpose so that we may fully complete our assignments here on Earth. –**Renée Cholmondeley**

PERSONAL REFLECTIONS

CHAPTER 3
THE GRIND, THE GRIEVING AND THE GRIEF

Despite the many setbacks throughout her young life, Ebonee pressed on with resilience and perseverance built on her strong faith in God.

REVIEW

What did you connect with the most from Ebonee's story? Why did that section from her story resonate with you? Share a moment when something similar happened to you.

TALK IT OUT

- Describe a situation where your insecurities hindered you from reaching a particular goal/goals?

- If you were able to overcome the situation, what worked? If not, what do you think you needed?

PERSONALIZE IT

- **Read Philippians 3:12 (NIV).** As business owners or as in life, we may encounter setbacks and distractions from our goals, but we must press on as in this Philippians verse. Describe the last time you had a problem in your life, and instead of going to others, you sought wisdom from God, and He gave it to you?

- Can you describe a time when you had to pour your heart out to the Lord?

TAKE ACTION

Recognize and record a moment recently when you brought God into a difficult situation.

Lady Insecurity had me withering into a deep hole within myself. She made me feel like there was nothing special about me and that I had nothing to offer the world. Even though she whispered in my ear often, I pressed on.
– **Ebonee Nicole-Lindsay**

PERSONAL REFLECTIONS

CHAPTER 4:

MY FAITH WALK TO ENTREPRENEURSHIP

Tamra's smooth move to Charlotte turned rocky when an abusive boyfriend followed her and refused to leave. After breaking up with him and landing an opportunity at a new company, the rug was pulled out from under her. She found herself with no family and no job. That desperation led her to step out on faith and into entrepreneurship.

REVIEW

What did you connect with the most from Tamra's story? Why did that section from her story resonate with you? Share a moment when something similar happened to you.

TALK IT OUT

- Describe a time when you knew you needed to walk away from an unhealthy friendship but felt obligated to stay connected?

- What was the turning point that made you say enough is enough and ended it? Were there any regrets? Discuss

PERSONALIZE IT

- **Read Ephesians 1:11 (NIV).** What's your first response when something unexpected happens to your plan?

- How are you doing at listening to God? What might be blocking your ability to hear Him?

TAKE ACTION

Do you believe that God always hears you? Why or why not?

I developed a strong conviction that I could make a valuable contribution to the world, and that I was born because there was something GOD needed me to do. I was sent here to provide information that my generation needs.
– **Tamra Tolbert-Bush**

PERSONAL REFLECTIONS

CHAPTER 5
THE LORD IS MY SHEPHERD

The 23rd Psalm has been a spiritual banner for Belinda. She always believed that the Lord was her personal guide in life, even when she was hit with setbacks, tragedies, and adversity. Through it all, she overcame and found her joy.

REVIEW

What did you connect with the most from Belinda's story? Why did that section from her story resonate with you? Share a moment when something similar happened to you.

TALK IT OUT

- What is something you like to be praised for?

- What helped you turn a recent problem into a praise?

PERSONALIZE IT

- **Read Psalm 23.** Share a challenge you have had to overcome by relying fully on God.

- How has God shown up in your life that makes you want to give back to Him?

TAKE ACTION

List three ways God has shown up for you when you were in a "wilderness" moment.

We can all touch lives every day, by a smile or helping hand. We are here to make a difference in someone's life. We can look to the example of Jesus to show us how to impact lives. The Lord is our Shepherd all day long. I hope my story will encourage you in your journey. All it takes is that one first step.

– **Belinda Spears**

PERSONAL REFLECTIONS

CHAPTER 6
IT TAKES A T.E.A.M.

Inspired by the death of a friend as a youth, C. Chinedu believed that anything could be achieved with **t**alented, **e**mpowered, and **a**spiring **m**en. So, he started the organization, T.E.A.M., while in college and watched as the principles he used helped the organization thrive. These principles continue to guide him to this day.

REVIEW

What did you connect with the most from C. Chinedu's story? Why did that section from her story resonate with you? Share a moment when something similar happened to you.

TALK IT OUT

- Talk about a time when you had to bring your best self to a situation.

- How did that behavior impact those around you?

PERSONALIZE IT

- **Read I Corinthians 12: 25-27 (NLT).** Can you describe a time when you had to work in a group and ended up stepping up as the leader?

- How did you put aside your own needs for the overall success of the team?

TAKE ACTION

List your strengths as it relates to working as part of a collaborative effort. Now ask two people who know you well to share their perceptions of your strengths. Compare the two lists. What did you learn?

Ultimately, I decided that I was the only person I could hold accountable to what had occurred in my community. I must be the change I want to see in this world. – **C. Chinedu Ifedi**

PERSONAL REFLECTIONS

CHAPTER 7

HOPE DEFERRED, BUT SUSTAINED BY FAITH

Stephanie's entrepreneurship journey has not been easy. The past several years have sometimes made her question her decision to become a business owner. Despite her struggles, she has kept her dreams alive, having faith that her success is deferred but not denied.

REVIEW

What did you connect with the most from Stephanie's story? Why did that section from her story resonate with you? Share a moment when something similar happened to you.

TALK IT OUT

- Would you describe your life currently as having more rainy days or more sunny days? Explain.

- Discuss situations in your life where you have been knocked down but had to get back up. How did you persevere?

PERSONALIZE IT

- **Read Proverbs 13:12 (TLB).** Have you ever experienced a time when you went before God and realized that you were doing all the talking and you needed to stop and listen? Explain.

- Have you ever felt that you spent more time asking God for more rather than acting on the gifts He has already provided? What's the solution?

TAKE ACTION

Read Matthew 7:7. How can you apply the "ask, seek and knock" concept to the gifts and talents that you possess? Write your answers.

My message to you is "Never give up!" Continue to lean into God. He sees you, He knows you. Most importantly, God LOVES YOU! You are needed to bring Heaven into this earth realm. – **Stephanie Morris**

PERSONAL REFLECTIONS

CHAPTER 8
E.S.C.A.P.E. TO CHARLOTTE

Rene always thought she would end up in California, but God had other plans for her. After receiving a vision that she was to create a mentoring program for girls, she watched amazed as God placed people and situations in her path to help her to champion that vision.

REVIEW

What did you connect with the most from Rene's story? Why did that section from her story resonate with you? Share a moment when something similar happened to you.

TALK IT OUT

- Share a time when you experienced God holding you, circling you with His affection.

- Were you able to stand strong, even though you were in a storm? Discuss.

PERSONALIZE IT

- **Read 2Timothy 1:12 (NIV).** What are some truths that have remained constant about you as it relates to persevering?

- How has God changed your heart about the way you view pain adversity? How did your view about God changes as a result?

TAKE ACTION

In what season of life have you seen God the clearest? Write your thoughts.

I have always known that my life would be a testimony, what I wasn't aware of is what I would have to go through for this testimony to manifest. – **Rene' Brewer**

PERSONAL REFLECTIONS

CHAPTER 9
FROM MAYBE TO YES.

With a perfect life and an ideal home in Michigan, Venita felt subtle shifts in the atmosphere around her doubled with answers to her prayers from God that felt like maybes. She now understands those shifts plus the maybes led to a loud yes, enabling her to use her divine gifting in alignment with her spirit.

REVIEW

What did you connect with the most from Venita's story? Why did that section from her story resonate with you? Share a moment when something similar happened to you.

TALK IT OUT

- Describe a time when you were tempted to overreact in a situation, but you handled it with grace.

- What was that like for you? What did you learn?

PERSONALIZE IT

- **Read Proverbs 22:29 (KJV).** This passage speaks to the idea that people who are truly talented; using their God-given gifts should serve those who appreciate their skills. Are you currently in an environment where your skills are being appreciated? If not, have you received any messages that you have ignored? What is stopping you from moving forward?

- Describe a time when your vulnerability deepened because of the pursuit of purpose.

TAKE ACTION

How do you reconcile leaving the comfort of what you know for the discomfort of the unknown?

I love the process of envisioning an idea, toying with it in my mind, tweaking, perfecting and ultimately bringing it to life.
– **Venita James**

PERSONAL REFLECTIONS

CHAPTER 10
DARE TO DREAM AGAIN

Through her story, Juanita teaches us that our first dream or vision for our life doesn't have to be our last. Sometimes the second dream makes way for God to bless us with a second chance.

REVIEW

What did you connect with the most from Juanita's story? Why did that section from her story resonate with you? Share a moment when something similar happened to you.

TALK IT OUT

- How does a secret shame keep you trapped?

- How has God carried you through a very difficult time?

PERSONALIZE IT

- **Read 1Peter 5:10 (NIV).** What is one area of healing you need to share with others?

- **Philippians 4:13 (NIV).** How did this healing allow you to move forward in your purpose?

TAKE ACTION

Are there any destructive behaviors or unhealthy patterns in any of your relationships? Take some time to write out a prayer asking the Lord to open your eyes to meaningful relationships.

Dream it. Write it down. Do it. Dream Again. You will be ready for your turn by turn steps, prepared to walk the path to your purpose. – **Juanita Corry Jackson**

PERSONAL REFLECTIONS

CHAPTER 11
PAIN TO PROSPERITY

Moreale's story is one of a woman in search of herself and her ultimate assignment. Moving from hard times to success, she endured many tragedies along the way. Despite the pain and trauma, she never lost sight of her purpose.

REVIEW

What did you connect with the most from Moreale's story? Why did that section resonate with you? Share a moment when something similar happened to you.

TALK IT OUT

- Why does honesty about pain and suffering drive some people away from God?

- Why is the prevailing thought that if something bad is happening to me, I must have done something bad to deserve it? Explain?

PERSONALIZE IT

- Read 2 Corinthians 2:2-3 (NIV). How is grief a sign of hope?

- How does remembering the hope of what's ahead for us help us deal with what we are presently walking through?

TAKE ACTION

Despite Moreale's experiences, she used her pain to inspire her journey to prosperity. Meditate on the scripture and journal about thoughts that may have bubbled up as a result.

Read Deuteronomy 8:18 (NLT). Take a few minutes to write down what God has done for you through your journey of pain to purpose. Share with the group.

However, it is faith and the desire to lead that keeps me pushing forward to my great destiny. I am a leader in God's eternal Kingdom, and I help others to lead. – **Moreale P Brown**

PERSONAL REFLECTIONS

CHAPTER 12
THE LILIES OF THE FIELD

For years Perkine struggled with the shame and disgrace of being molested by a family friend at a young age. Over time and with a great deal of personal success, she found the courage to share her story with her mother which gave her peace and started her journey to healing.

REVIEW

What did you connect with the most from Perkine's story? Why did that section resonate with you? Share a moment when something similar happened to you.

TALK IT OUT

- Describe a time when you have been hurt and the pain led to self-sabotage.

- How were your relationships impacted?

PERSONALIZE IT

- Share a way you pretend in order to forget a painful past.

- Do you feel that the pain you have experienced in life has put distance between you and God or prompted you to lean into him more fully?

TAKE ACTION

Matthew 6:28-33 (NIV). Spend a few moments meditating on these verses. List ways you can reconcile with past shame and hurts.

My God sent signs of wonder to me. These signs let me know that I was special in His sight even though I did not feel his immediate presence. – **Perkine Denoyes-Theus**

PERSONAL REFLECTIONS

PERSONAL REFLECTIONS

PERSONAL REFLECTIONS

PERSONAL REFLECTIONS

BIO

JOAN T RANDALL is an award-winning, bestselling author, certified speaker, coach, and domestic violence victim's advocate whose mission is to impact lives to change the outcomes.

ANGELA M HAIGLER is an author, freelance writer/editor and writing coach. Her book reviews and articles can be found in regional and national publications.

www.ingramcontent.com/pod-product-compliance
Lightning Source LLC
Chambersburg PA
CBHW071457070426
42452CB00040B/1549